D1784286

## A Note from the Author

Inspired by my 6 nieces and nephews, along with time spent studying and working as a Marine biologist, I created the "Animal Stories" series, with its bright, colourful pictures, child friendly words and scientifically accurate information, I hope everyone enjoys exploring the underwater world with Anna and her friends.

Jon

## Note to Parents, Guardians, Nursery Nurses, Teachers and Other Professionals

The Animal Stories series of books has been written and illustrated with a variety of special educational needs in mind;

- The font used throughout the books is "Dyslexie" and has been specially created to aid people with dyslexia to read easier, faster and with fewer mistakes.
- The repetition of words and phrases along with the language used is intended to help new readers recognise words and aid reading.
- The bold colours and simple illustrations, combined with the limited number of words per page and relatively short stories are designed to keep the interest of those with short attention spans like ADHD sufferers

Alongside all of the above, the simple biologically accurate stories and "The Biology Bit" at the end of each book, are designed to spark interest in the natural world and its ongoing conservation and protection for future generations to enjoy.

# Anna the Anglerfish

## Written and illustrated
## by Jon Adams

This is Anna the Anglerfish, Anna lives deep in the sea where it is very cold, very dark, very scary and very boring

One day Anna said, "I do not like living deep in the sea anymore, it is too cold, dark, scary and boring". So she slowly started swimming upwards.

As Anna was swimming up, she bumped into Terry the Toothfish.

Anna said, "Hi Terry, it is too dark, scary, cold and boring in the deep sea, and I do not like it anymore, so I am swimming up to the surface".

Terry said, "Silly Anna, we deep sea animals have special blood with anti-freeze in it, so we do not get cold".

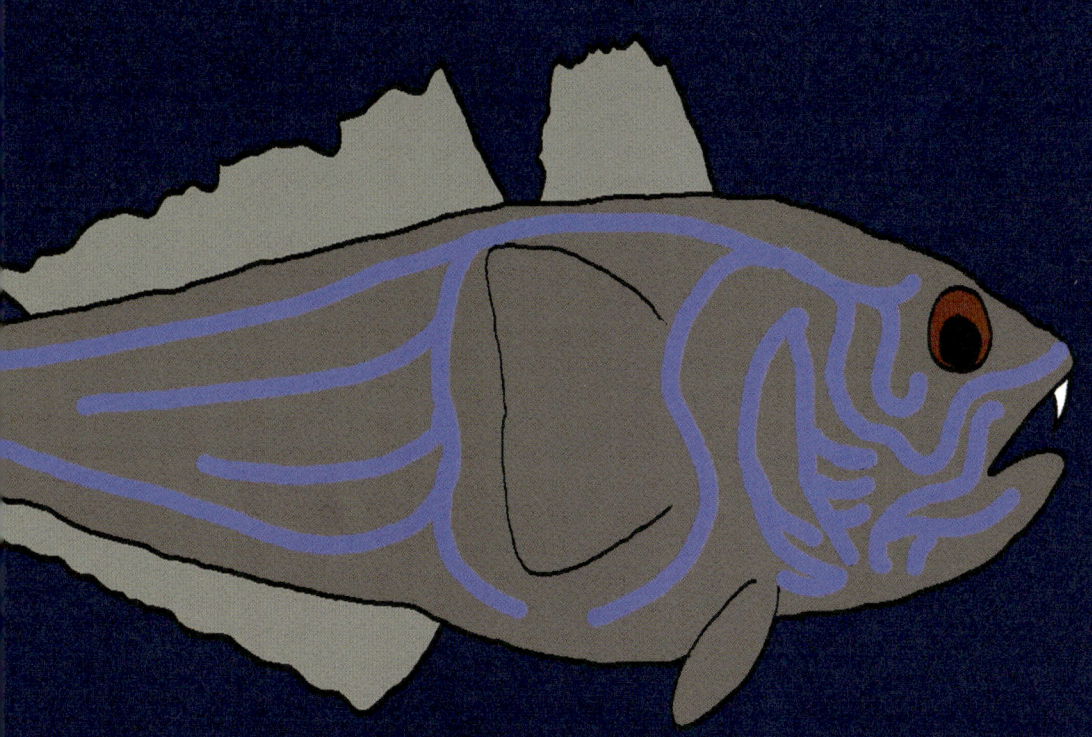

Anna stopped swimming and started to think.

Soon Anna said, "You are right Terry, I had forgotten about my special blood, but it is still too dark, scary and boring in the deep sea".

So she started to swim up again.

Soon Anna bumped into Sarah the Squirrelfish.

Anna said, "Hi Sarah, it is too dark, scary and boring in the deep sea, and I do not like it anymore, so I am swimming up to the surface".

Sarah said, "Silly Anna, we deep sea animals have really big eyes to help us see in the dark".

Anna stopped swimming and
started to think.

Soon Anna said, "You are right Sarah,
I had forgotten about my big eyes,
but it is still too scary and boring in
the deep sea".

So she started to swim up again.

As Anna was swimming up, she bumped into Jack the Jellyfish.

Anna said, "Hi Jack, it is too dark, scary and boring in the deep sea, and I do not like it anymore, so I am swimming up to the surface".

Jack said, "Silly Anna, lots of deep sea animals like you and me can light up parts of their bodies and scare off anything scary".

Anna stopped swimming and
started to think.

Soon Anna said, "You are right Jack, I had forgotten about my special light, but it is still too boring in the deep sea".

So she started to swim up again.

Soon Anna was at the top of the sea and she stopped swimming and had a look around.

Then Anna thought, "It is definitely not too cold or too dark at the top of the sea, in fact it is too hot and bright".

Just then lots of little fish came swimming past Anna very fast.

Anna thought, "It is not scary at the top of the sea, but it is very busy".

As Anna was thinking Sid the Squid came swimming past.

Sid said, "Cheer up Anna, you look sad, what is wrong?"

Anna said, "Hi Sid, I am sad, I do not like living in the deep sea anymore, it is too cold, too dark, too scary and too boring so I swam to the top of the sea, but it is too hot, too bright and too busy at the top of the sea".

Sid said, "Anna, the deep sea is not boring I love going to the deep sea, it is full of really unusual and interesting things! Follow me and I will show you".

So Anna followed Sid back down to the deep sea, past Jack the Jellyfish

# Past Sarah the Squirrelfish

Past Terry the Toothfish, right to the very bottom of the sea.

Anna said, "Sid it is still too dark, I can not see anything interesting in the deep sea".

Sid said, "Turn on your special light and tell me if it is still boring in the deep sea".

So Anna turned on her special light and looked around. All around her Anna saw interesting things, there were strange shaped and coloured animals all around her...

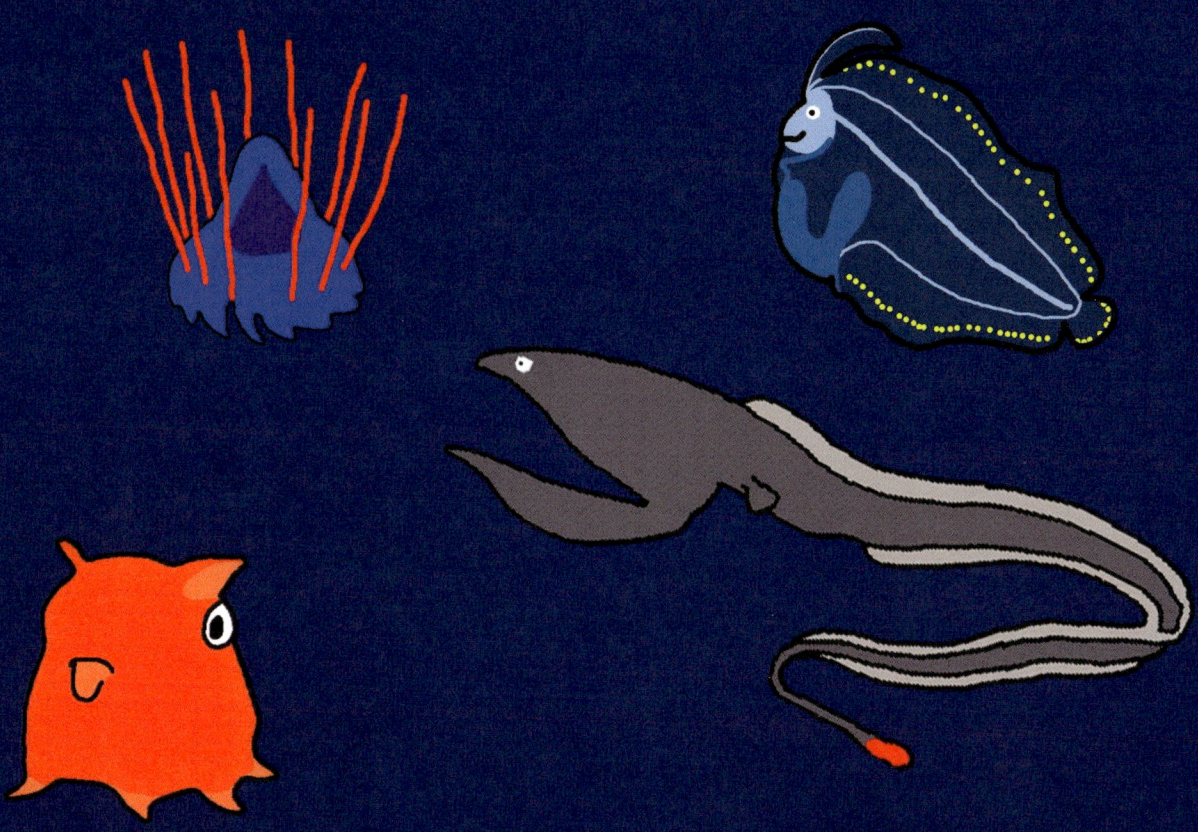

And strange looking rocks that looked as if they had smoke coming out of them, in fact it was not boring at all!

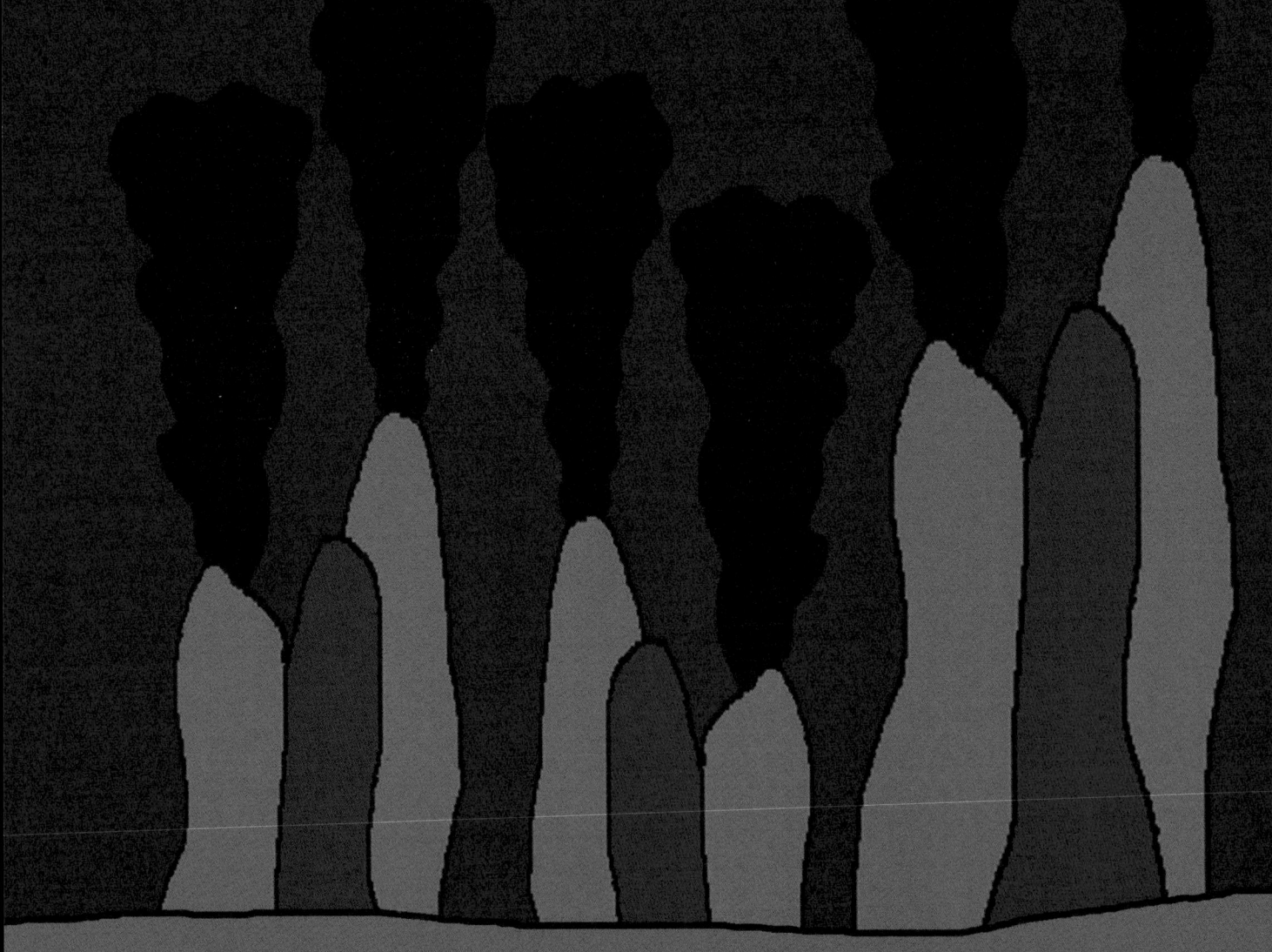

Anna said, "Wow thanks Sid, I had never seen all this before, if only I had turned on my special light I would not have been bored at all!"

Anna swam off looking at all the interesting things and making lots of new friends.

# The Biology Bit

• All the animals found in "Anna the Anglerfish" are based on animals found in the deep sea. The characters are limited to family groups not individual species as many animal families (like crabs) share characteristics across the globe meaning the same characters can be used across the Animal Stories series.

• Anna the Anglerfish is a Kroyer's Deep Sea Anglerfish (Ceratias holboelli).

• Terry the Toothfish is a Patagonian Toothfish (Dissostichus eleginoides).

• Sarah the Squirrelfish is a Longspine Squirrelfish (Holocentrus rufus).

• Jack the Jellyfish is a Barrel Jellyfish (Rhizostome plumo).

• Sid the Squid is a Humboldt Squid (Dosidicus gigas).

• All the animals in Anna the Anglerfish are deep sea specialists.
There are a variety of methods animals has used to adapt to the dark, cold and pressurised deep sea. In general they have huge eyes in comparison to their size, most have special blood containing an organic antifreeze, and many can also produce light through bioluminesance in one way or another to search for prey or scare a predator.

• In truth, biologists are still only scratching the tip of a very large iceberg regarding how the various animals have adapted, in fact each time they look for one species they will often find more species never seen by science and not find the species they were looking for in the first place.
It is hard to believe but we know more about the surface of the moon and space than we do of the deep oceans here on planet Earth.

# Also Available.

Chris the Crab
by Jon Adams

Tina the Tang
by Jon Adams

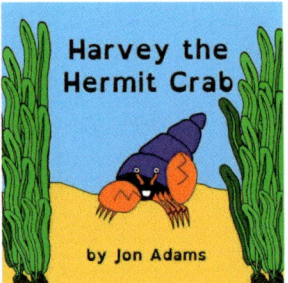
Harvey the Hermit Crab
by Jon Adams

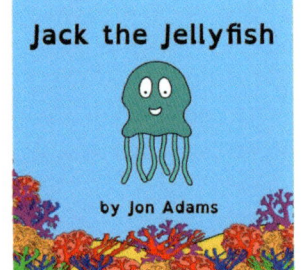
Jack the Jellyfish
by Jon Adams

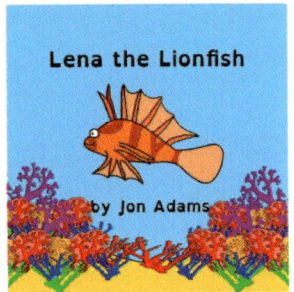
Lena the Lionfish
by Jon Adams

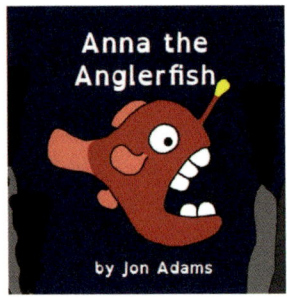
Anna the Anglerfish
by Jon Adams

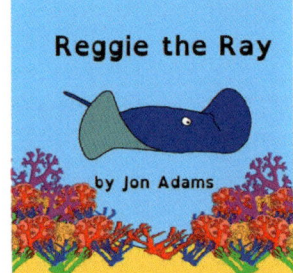
Reggie the Ray
by Jon Adams

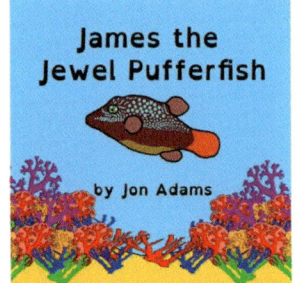
James the Jewel Pufferfish
by Jon Adams

Bo the Beluga Whale
by Jon Adams

Debbie the Dolphin
by Jon Adams

Steve the Starfish
by Jon Adams

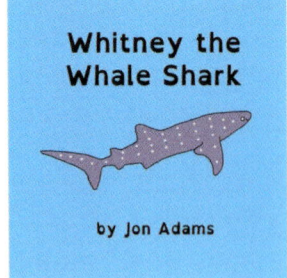
Whitney the Whale Shark
by Jon Adams

Visit www.Animal-Stories.co.uk for the latest on the Sea Stories Series.

33831577R00020

Printed in Great Britain
by Amazon